Fun on Wheels

Peter Sloan

Momentum
Fun on Wheels

First published in Great Britain in 1998 by

Folens Publishers
Albert House
Apex Business Centre
Boscombe Road
Dunstable
Beds LU5 4RL

© 1998 Momentum developed by Barrie Publishing Pty Limited
Suite 513, 89 High St, Kew, Vic 3101, Australia

Peter Sloan hereby asserts his moral right to be identified as the author
of this work in accordance with the Copyright, Designs and Patents Act
1988.
© 1998 Folens Ltd. on behalf of the author.

British Library Cataloguing in Publication Data.
A Catalogue record for this book is available from the British Library

ISBN 1 86202 400 6

Designed by Tom Kurema
Printed in Singapore by PH Productions Pte Ltd

Every effort has been made to contact the owners of the photographs in
this book. Where this has not been possible, we invite the owners of the
copyright to notify the publishers.

S. & T. Clarke cover, pp. 12, 13; Tony Feder/Sporting Pix p. 15;
Greg Ford/Sporting Pix pp. 1, 7, 8, 9, 10, 11;
Stuart Milligan/Sporting Pix p. 5; B. Silkstone cover, pp. 5, 6;
Sporting Pix pp. 3, 4; Sutton/Sporting Pix pp. 4, 14, 15.

Ever since they were invented, motor vehicles have been used for fun and for racing. There are all kinds of cars and many varieties of car racing. For some kinds of races, the drivers need to be very skilled, as racing cars in these races can be dangerous. There are other kinds of car races that are not so dangerous and can be enjoyed by everyone.

Formula One racing cars are very high-powered cars. They are expensive to make because they have special bodies and engines.

These very fast cars are driven only on race tracks. Formula One drivers need special skills to drive at such high speeds.

Touring cars are made by changing the cars that people drive on the roads. Some touring cars have been changed so much it is hard to tell what sort of cars they were to begin with. People like to watch touring car racing because it is fast and there are often big crashes.

Drag racers are unusual cars. They are made to go as fast as possible in the shortest time. Drag racers have very powerful engines and use a special fuel. These cars have large rear tyres and sometimes use a parachute to stop them. When drag racers race, they go in a straight line, very fast, for only a few seconds.

Go-karts are small cars that sit very close to the ground. Go-karts have small motors, but they can go quite fast and are fun to race on short tracks. They are very safe to drive. There are special go-kart tracks where boys and girls can have fun racing.

Moto-cross bikes are motor bikes used for riding on dirt tracks. These bikes are light and strong. They have special tires that can grip well in mud, in sand, or on rocky trails. Moto-cross bikes are great bikes for having fun, and riders need to know how to do a lot of tricks to be able to ride on some of the best trails.

There are small and large-sized bikes to choose from, and riders must keep their bikes in good repair and know how to look after them. Many moto-cross bikers belong to a club where they learn how to ride well and safely.

Rally cars compete by going to different places over a long distance in a short time. Rallies are often held in country areas. A special route has to be followed. The route is usually over rough roads under very difficult conditions. Rally cars need to be strong and carefully prepared. Only certain kinds of changes can be made to a basic road car to classify it as a rally car.

Index